Maria Martinez
Pueblo Potter

Maria Martinez

"We don't care about being well known or anything. Pueblo Indian people don't think about things like that. We all just want to get along in the world and be together."

Maria Martinez
Pueblo Potter

By Peter Anderson

CHILDRENS PRESS ®
CHICAGO

PHOTO CREDITS

Museum of New Mexico: cover; signature, cover; 1, 13, 24;
    Tyler Dingee, 2, 3, 11 (top right, bottom left, bottom
    right), 12 (left and right); John K. Hillers, 5; Harold
    Kellogg, 6, 25; Wesley Bradfield, 7; Wyatt Davis, 8, 9, 11
    (top left), 17 (top), 19; T. Harmon Parkhurst, 18, 29;
    David Stein, 20; Arthur Taylor, 21 (left and right), 28 (left
    and right); Jesse Nusbaum, 22; William H. Regan, 30
    (left); Maurice Eby, 30 (right), 32
David Hiser, Photographer/Aspen: 15
Museum of the American Indian, New York City: 16
Earthscenes, ©C. Prescott-Allen: 17 (left)
Barbara Gonzales: 27
Jerry Jacka: 31

EDITORIAL STAFF

Project Editor: E. Russell Primm III
Design and Electronic Composition: Biner Design
Photo Research: Carol Parden
Editorial Assistance: Ann Duvall

ACKNOWLEDGEMENTS

The author and editors would like to thank Stephen
Trimble for his review of the manuscript. His critical eye
and expertise on Pueblo pottery were valuable additions.

Library of Congress Cataloging-in-Publication Data
Anderson, Peter, 1956–
    Maria Martinez: Pueblo potter / by Peter Anderson
        p. cm. (Picture story biography)
    Summary: Describes the life and accomplishment of the
Pueblo Indian woman who made pottery in the traditional
way of her people and achieved renown as an artist.
        ISBN 0-516-04184-3
    1. Martinez, Maria Montoya — Juvenile literature. 2.
Tewa Indians — Pottery — Juvenile literature. 3. Tewa
Indians — Biography — Juvenile literature. 4. San
Ildefonso (N.M.) — Juvenile literature. [1. Martinez, Maria
Montoya. 2. Artists. 3. Pueblo Indians — Biography. 4.
Indians of North America — New Mexico — Biography.] I.
Title. II. Series: Picture-story biographies.
E99.S213M374 1992   92-4807
738'.092 — dc20   CIP
[B]   AC
AC

San Ildefonso Pueblo, New Mexico, about 1880

THE DAY DAWNED calm and clear over the Pueblo Indian village of San Ildefonso, New Mexico. The February air was still — not a wisp of wind. It was the kind of day Maria Martinez had been waiting for. She gathered the clay pots she had made. Today, she would bake them in the fire till they were hard. Only a calm day like this would do. If wind blew the smoke sideways, it would smudge the polished clay.

5

Maria carried the pottery out to the firepit behind her home. Nicolasa, Maria's aunt, brought over some of the pots that she had made. Together, they carefully placed their pots and jars in the firepit. First, they covered them with large pieces of broken pottery to shield them from the flames. Then, they added layers of cedar sticks and manure.

As a child Maria had learned that the clay and water which she used to make her pots were gifts from the earth. Now, as they prepared for the firing, Nicolasa said a prayer. She asked that the pottery

Maria carefully placed the jars and pots in the firepit for firing.

*Maria's empty firepit ready
for more pottery to be fired*

turn out well. She sprinkled cornmeal over the firepit. This was the Pueblo way of giving thanks back to the earth. "Now it is time," she said.

Julian, Maria's husband, lit the fire. A straight line of smoke rose up through the pinyon pine and juniper trees that surrounded the Martinez house. It rose up over the cluster of mud-brick homes that made up the village of San Ildefonso. It rose higher still over the brownish-green hills and mesas that rimmed the valley. As wind and water had shaped these hills and mesas, so Maria and Nicolasa had shaped their clay. On this February morning back in 1909, as the smoke drifted into the turquoise sky, they waited for the fire to bake their pots.

Making pots was nothing new for Maria. Born in the early 1880s, she began to work with clay as a young girl. With her sister Desideria, she dug clay to make a playhouse. The soft, gooey clay made good mortar for their rock walls and fireplaces. And it was just right for making dishes to play

The people of San Ildefonso Pueblo use the same clay to make both the walls of their buildings and their pottery.

Nicolasa, Maria's aunt, showed her how to mix the right amounts of sand and clay.

with. But when the clay dried, their dishes always cracked. Maria went to her aunt to find out why.

Watching Nicolasa work, Maria learned how to mix the clay with volcanic ash and water so that it held together. She learned to keep her clay moist while shaping it. She learned how to dip her fingers in water and smooth the surface of the clay. Most important, she learned that the knowledge and skill needed to make good pottery was something to be shared.

For many generations, that was the way it had been. To learn a craft, young people would watch their elders at work. Then they would try it on their own. In this way, making pots linked one generation to the next.

So it was with Maria Martinez. She learned to make pots the way her ancestors had made them. To begin, she would gather the clay and ash. Then came many hours of grinding and cleaning this mixture until it was fine and smooth. Next she would knead the clay, as if making a loaf of bread. Then she pressed the clay pancake into a shallow bowl to shape the base of her pot. Onto this base she coiled pieces of clay. These pieces of clay made the walls of the pot. Maria shaped the walls with a scraper made from a piece of gourd. Then she

(top left) Maria prepares the clay before she begins shaping the pots and jars. This process can be very time consuming. (top right) After the clay is prepared, a "pancake" is rolled out for the pottery base. (bottom left) Next coils of clay are added to the base to make the walls. (bottom right) Maria used a scraper to smooth the sides of the pottery.

(left) A mixture of clay and water, called slip, is then applied to the pottery. (right) Finally, Maria used special polishing stones to rub the pottery smooth and shiny.

painted on a mixture of clay and water called slip. Using special polishing stones, Maria rubbed the pot until it was shiny and smooth. Her husband Julian often painted designs on the pot. Then it would be ready to fire.

In this way, Maria carried on a Pueblo tradition. For hundreds of years, Pueblo Indians had made pottery from the clay found around their high desert homes. As early as 500 A.D., their ancestors, a group of Indians referred to as the Anasazi, or "Ancient Ones," had made pottery in much the same way.

The Anasazi were of great interest to a group of archaeologists who were uncovering an Anasazi village near San Ildefonso. As they dug deeper, they hoped to gather more information about these mysterious Indians of the past.

Pueblo men helped archaeologists uncover the history of the Anasazi at dig sites.

One day, the archaeologists came to San Ildefonso looking for men to help them dig. Julian, like other Pueblo men, was glad for the work. After several years of drought, followed by a year of flooding and erosion, few Pueblo families were able to live off their crops. Many Pueblo men had to find work elsewhere, sometimes a long way from home. The dig was a chance for Julian to make a living without going too far away.

So Julian joined the team of archaeologists during the summer of 1908. He was curious about the Anasazi. He was especially interested in the pictures that they had etched and painted onto the walls of nearby caves and canyons. Before long, Julian had filled a notebook with drawings of Anasazi rock art.

One day, later that summer, Dr. Edgar Lee Hewett, the head archaeologist, came to Maria with pieces of pottery uncovered at the dig. Maria examined the pottery pieces. They were thin, hard, and shiny. Black lines painted on the dark gray pieces made an unusual pattern. Dr. Hewett asked her if she could make this kind of pottery. "I never saw this kind of pottery made," said Maria, "but I can try. I can't make the designs, though . . . I don't know how to draw." Having noticed Julian's

Examples of pottery made by the "Ancient Ones," the Anasazi

15

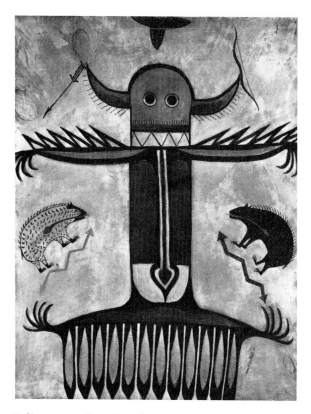

Julian not only painted on pottery but also on animal skins.
This painting is done in watercolors and was finished in 1922.

artistic talents, Dr. Hewett suggested
that he paint the designs. "All right,"
said Maria, "we can try."

Maria knew about the fine-grained
ash that made the clay so hard. So one
winter day, she and Julian rode out in
their wagon and filled a couple of flour
sacks full of this ash. On the way
home, Julian collected the sharp

narrow leaves of several yucca plants.
By chewing on the end of these leaves,
he made paintbrushes. Using different
colored clays and a shrub called
beeplant, he made paint.

(top) Julian gathered the clay that Maria later mixed with sand to make into pottery. (left) The brushes that Julian used to paint the pottery were made from yucca plants such as these.

Maria sifted the fine ash through a piece of cloth, mixing it with clay and water. From this mixture, she shaped a bowl. And onto the bowl, Julian painted the design of a serpent, much like one he had seen in a cave near the dig site. Maria made several more pots until she ran out of her special clay. Then it was a matter of waiting for the

Julian painted Maria's pottery with a yucca brush.

After the firing had hardened the pottery, Julian removed the pots and jars from the firepit.

right time to bake them in the fire. The time finally came one bright blue February morning.

As the fire smoldered underneath a layer of finely ground manure, Maria used a pair of sticks to lift the first piece of pottery out of the ashes. As she blew the ashes off this jar, Julian lifted the rest of the pots from the fire.

19

*An example of Maria's
first pieces of pottery*

Three of the five pieces Maria had made
came out perfectly. Like the pot pieces
Dr. Hewett had given her, they were
dark with darker lines where Julian had
painted on the designs. But the other
two pots were black all over. Maybe
they had been too close to the fire, she
thought. Without thinking much more
about these black pots, Maria stored
them away. When Dr. Hewett came to
visit the following summer, she showed
him only the pottery that turned out as
she had planned.

Dr. Hewett was impressed. He bought all three of Maria's pieces and offered to help her sell more of her work. When Julian took a job working for Dr. Hewett at a museum in Santa Fe later that fall, Maria went with him. They sold their pots to museum visitors. Before long their pots caught the attention of a local shopkeeper. The shopkeeper was interested in selling Maria's pots too. Before long, she was selling her work faster than she could make it.

(below, left and right) Examples of Maria Martinez's early light-colored pottery. The designs were painted by her husband, Julian.

One day, when the shopkeeper came by to ask her for more pots, she told him she had run out. She told him that some of the other women at San Ildefonso had made some nice pots. But the shopkeeper said that he only wanted Maria's work. Maria didn't understand. Why should it matter that a particular woman made a pot? What mattered was that the pot came from San Ildefonso. She finally convinced

Maria and two women from San Ildefonso demonstrated Pueblo pottery techniques at the Palace of the Governors in Santa Fe, New Mexico, about 1912.

the shopkeeper to sell some pots that her sisters had made.

While Maria made more pots, Julian went back to San Ildefonso to gather up some of the ones that Maria's sisters had made. When he returned, he brought along the black pots that Maria had hidden away in her storeroom. "The black pots!" she said. "The ones that were spoiled. We can't sell those!" But Julian figured they should try. What did they have to lose?

The next morning, when the shopkeeper returned, Julian told him that they had some special pots to sell. These pots, he said, were different from any others that had been made at San Ildefonso. He showed the black pots to the shopkeeper. "Those are different all right," the shopkeeper said. For a long time, the shopkeeper examined the black pots. "I like them," he finally said.

As it turned out, so did his customers. The black pots sold out faster than any of the others. The shopkeeper wanted more right away, so Julian and Maria got right to work. Maria shaped the clay and Julian built the fires. When the firing was almost done, he smothered the flames with manure and blackened the pots.

Other Pueblo Indians at Santa Clara and other villages had made black pottery before. But none of their pots had the shiny polished look that made

Maria and Julian worked long hours to keep up with the demand for their pottery.

During the firing process the pottery is covered with cedar sticks and manure.

Maria's work so popular. In 1913, after several years of spending much of her time at the museum, Maria moved back to San Ildefonso. By then, her pots were well known. Soon orders were coming in from all over the country. More and more visitors came to buy her pots. Maria soon realized she needed a store of her own. So Julian built an addition onto their house. There, he decorated Maria's pots and sold their work to visitors.

As the demand for San Ildefonso pottery grew, Maria was pleased to share her knowledge with other women in her village. Just as Nicolasa had taught her, Maria believed that pottery making was a gift to all of her people. She was glad that others in the community were learning the craft. She was glad that they set up their own shops for visitors to the village. Maybe that would give her a chance to keep up with all the mail orders.

By now, making pots was something that kept Maria's whole family busy. Her sisters helped shape the clay. Julian continued firing the pots, running the store, and painting the designs. But it wasn't until 1919 that he found a way to paint designs on her black pottery. Using the slip that Maria had polished with, he added his touch to one of Maria's finished pots. When

Maria and her family gathered together in San Ildefonso Pueblo

*(left and above) Samples of Maria's famous
"black-on-black" style pottery*

they took it out of the fire, it was shiny
black except for the dull black lines
where Julian had painted.

This new style of pottery, known now
as "black-on-black," won Maria and her
family many honors. Over the years,
Maria was invited to display her work at
World's Fairs in St. Louis, San Diego,
Chicago, and San Francisco. Later on,
three different universities awarded her
honorary degrees. Perhaps one of
Maria's most memorable honors came in
1934 when she was invited to visited the

White House for the first time. Eleanor Roosevelt, the President's wife, gave a moving speech to Maria and other Indian artists. Mrs. Roosevelt said that Indian art was a priceless part of our American heritage that could never be replaced. She encouraged the artists to keep their traditions alive.

Maria did just that. Much to her credit, the tradition lives on at the village of San Ildefonso today. Throughout her life, Maria continued

Maria and Julian teaching some of the other Pueblo Indians at San Ildefonso the art of pottery making

to develop her art, sharing the creation
of her pots with other members of her
family. After Julian died in 1943,
Santana, Maria's sister-in-law, became
her helper. And in 1956, she began
working with Popovi Da, her son. Maria
retired from making pottery in 1971, but
she continued to share her knowledge
until her death in 1980.

*(left) After Julian died, Maria's sister-in-law Santana
became her helper and painted the designs on the
pottery. (below) Popovi Da, Maria's son, also worked
with Maria in making and decorating the pottery.*

Maria holds one of her black-on-black pots in San Ildefonso

Shaping clay, Maria believed, was all about sharing. In taking the old ways of her ancestors and passing them on, Maria shared the traditions of the Pueblos. In creating with water and clay, she took the gifts of the earth and made them her own. Then she gave them back — to her family, to her neighbors in San Ildefonso, and to the many people who came to admire her works of clay.

Maria Martinez

Index

About the Author

Peter Anderson studied Native American literature and history while earning an M.A. in American Studies at the University of Wyoming. He has worked as a carpenter, editor, river guide, and newspaper reporter. Currently he lives in Salt Lake City where he teaches part-time and writes. During the summer, he is a wilderness ranger with the U.S. Forest Service. Mr. Anderson's other books for Childrens Press include *Will Rogers: American Humorist* and *Charles Eastman: Physician, Reformer, and Native American Leader*.

JB Martinez
Anderson, Peter, 1956-
  Maria Martinez

DATE DUE			